GUIDES TO RESPONSIBLE HUNTING

PREPARING AND ENJOYING A MEAL YOU HUNTED

GUIDES TO RESPONSIBLE HUNTING

GUIDES TO RESPONSIBLE HUNTING
PREPARING AND ENJOYING A MEAL YOU HUNTED

By Elizabeth Dee

MASON CREST

Mason Crest
450 Parkway Drive, Suite D
Broomall, Pennsylvania 19008
(866) MCP-BOOK (toll-free)
www.masoncrest.com

First printing
9 8 7 6 5 4 3 2 1
Printed in the USA

ISBN (hardback) 978-1-4222-4100-4
ISBN (series) 978-1-4222-4097-7
ISBN (ebook) 978-1-4222-7699-0

Library of Congress Cataloging-in-Publication Data
Names: Dee, Elizabeth, 1957- author.
Title: Preparing and enjoying a meal you hunted / Elizabeth Dee.
Description: Broomall, Pennsylvania : Mason Crest, [2019] | Series: Guides for responsible hunting
Identifiers: LCCN 2018006641 (print) | LCCN 2018002320 (ebook) | ISBN 9781422276990 (eBook) |
ISBN 9781422241004 (hardback) | ISBN 9781422240977 (series) | ISBN 9781422276990 (ebook)
Subjects: LCSH: Hunting. | Cooking (Game)
Classification: LCC SK33 (print) | LCC SK33 .D44 2019 (ebook) | DDC 639/.1--dc23
LC record available at https://lccn.loc.gov/2018006641

Developed and Produced by National Highlights Inc.
Editor: Keri De Deo
Interior and cover design: Priceless Digital Media
Production: Michelle Luke

CONTENTS

KEY ICONS TO LOOK FOR:

 Words to Understand: These words with their easy-to-understand definitions will increase the reader's understanding of the text while building vocabulary skills.

 Sidebars: This boxed material within the main text allows readers to build knowledge, gain insights, explore possibilities, and broaden their perspectives by weaving together additional information to provide realistic and holistic perspectives.

 Educational Videos: Readers can view videos by scanning our QR codes, providing them with additional educational content to supplement the text. Examples include news coverage, moments in history, speeches, iconic sports moments and much more!

 Text-Dependent Questions: These questions send the reader back to the text for more careful attention to the evidence presented there.

 Research Projects: Readers are pointed toward areas of further inquiry connected to each chapter. Suggestions are provided for projects that encourage deeper research and analysis.

 Series Glossary of Key Terms: This back-of-the book glossary contains terminology used throughout this series. Words found here increase the reader's ability to read and comprehend higher-level books and articles in this field.

5

 Words to Understand:

field dressing: In the wild, butchering and preparing meat for eating.

gutting: To remove the body organs from inside an animal.

hide: The skin of an animal.

skinning: To remove the skin from an animal.

venison: Deer meat.

CHAPTER 1
CLEANING

Wild game, like wild turkey legs, is lean and healthy meat.

Wild game is some of the healthiest meat on the planet. Consider deer meat, or **venison**, for example. Not only does venison contain very little fat, but it's "free-range" meat. That means deer meat contains none of the antibiotics, growth hormones, or other chemicals like commercially-grown beef, pork, or poultry. Deer eat only organic food in the wild their whole life. Venison is as natural as food gets! The same goes for rabbit and bird meat. Animals that are hunted and harvested in the wild are one of the healthiest forms of meat for humans to eat.

HARVESTING YOUR ANIMAL FOR FOOD

Use a special knife for field dressing game.

Although some hunters take their animals to be processed by a commercial facility, you can do it yourself in the field. **Field dressing** makes transporting meat back to camp or home a lot easier because you only take the edible parts and leave the rest for scavengers.

You will need to check the regulations and hunting laws in your state or province to find out if you are allowed to leave deer remains in the wild, or ask your parent to check for you. Some areas only require that you don't dump deer remains on the side of the road. It is considered littering.

When field dressing a deer or other animal, such as a rabbit, always make sure the animal is dead and not merely wounded. Accompanied by an adult, carefully approach the animal and prod it with a stick. Watch for any eye movement or signs of breathing. If the animal is still alive, you must shoot it again to keep it from suffering any further. Shooting through the heart is the quickest way.

How to Smoke Venison Deer Meat.

FIELD DRESSING SUPPLIES YOU WILL NEED

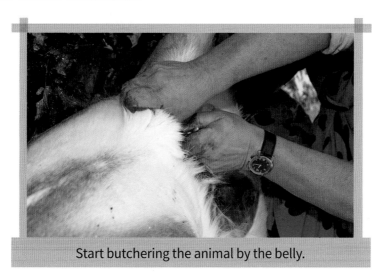

Start butchering the animal by the belly.

Always wear latex gloves when field dressing a wild animal. Use a knife dedicated to the task. Don't use a kitchen knife that you will use in the preparation of other food at home because the tool will be contaminated. Using one knife only for field dressing prevents the spread of disease if an animal is infected. For example, a deer may have chronic wasting disease.

A pair of large scissors is useful for cutting away the tough membrane. Use a small saw for cutting through bone.

You will need a roll of paper towels for this task and an assortment of plastic bags for the different cuts of meat, such as roasts, spare ribs, tenderloins, and even the heart and liver if you desire. Use a black permanent marker to label the bags. Be careful not to smear the ink until it dries.

Be sure to have some salt on hand as a rub for the meat to aid in preservation. A big plastic bucket makes it easier to carry the packages of meat out of the field. It's essential to field dress an animal as quickly as possible after shooting it. Removing the body organs such as the bladder and intestines keeps the meat from acquiring a bad taste.

CAREFUL WITH THOSE SHARP KNIVES!

 Young hunters should not field dress any animal without adult help and supervision. Large animals can be very heavy and awkward to handle alone, plus you will be using very sharp knives and scissors to cut away the hide, connective tissue, and the internal organs.

When gutting and skinning a deer or other animal, be very careful with sharp knives, scissors, or saws. You don't want to risk getting a deep cut while out in the wild, perhaps miles from a medical facility. Just take your time and don't get in a hurry. Be sure to have an adult to assist you and guide you through the process. If this is your first time field dressing an animal, do more watching of the process than participating and be sure to ask a lot of questions!

Be sure you carry a first aid kit, equipped with plenty of clean bandage material and surgical tape, not just small adhesive bandages for small cuts or abrasions. Include anti-bacterial ointment and a tourniquet kit as well, just to be safe.

You should also be careful when hanging up a large animal carcass for field dressing or any other location. You don't want to strain muscles or sustain an injury by trying to lift a weight that is too heavy for your body to handle. Always ask an adult, or several adults to help, if necessary.

SPLITTING OPEN THE CARCASS

Field dressing requires a lot of equipment. Plan carefully.

To make the process of field dressing easier to understand, the steps outlined below will focus on how to process a deer. However, you can easily apply the same process to other animals and even birds.

For the first step, make sure you work on flat ground, especially with a larger animal such as a deer or elk. Place the animal on its back to expose the belly. Some hunters hang deer upside down in a tree for **gutting**. Other hunters prefer to hang a deer by its head for the process. Either method allows the blood to drain out of the carcass. You can also purchase a metal folding tripod for this purpose.

To hang a deer by the hind legs, you will need to make a slit between the main leg bone on the ankle and the large tendon that runs behind it. Do this on both legs. Slide a metal bar or wooden pole through these slits. The deer can then be hoisted up and hung using a rope or chain attached to the middle of the bar or pole.

EQUIPMENT NEEDED TO FIELD DRESS AN ANIMAL

Decide early if you want to keep the head for mounting.

- **Latex gloves**

- **Hand sanitizer**

- **Water**

- **First aid kit**

- One knife for gutting

- One extra knife

- Large scissors

- Small saw

- Paper towels

- Plastic bags - assorted sizes for cuts of meat

- Black marker

- Big plastic bucket

- Salt

- Plastic trash bag to collect used paper towels and gloves for disposal

ADDITIONAL EQUIPMENT IF DESIRED

- Game cart for transporting carcass

- Some form of cord or rope

- Wooden dowel or strong stick

- Portable tripod for hanging up animal

DECIDE NOW IF YOU WANT THE HEAD MOUNTED

If you plan to save the head to be mounted by a taxidermist, you should hang the deer by the hind legs. Hanging a deer by its head could cause a lot of damage to the head and neck, making the specimen unfit for mounting. Hanging a deer by its antlers should also be avoided to prevent damage if you want the head mounted.

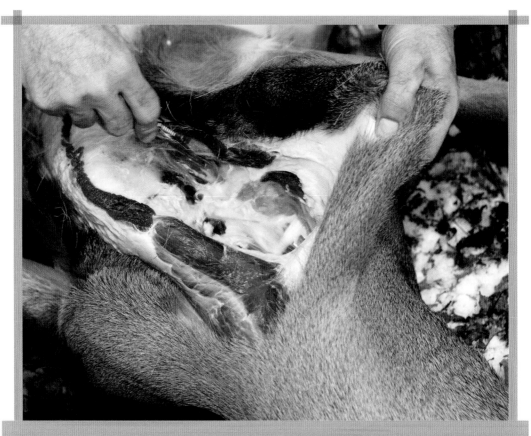

Cleaning wild game takes precision and skill.

YOU WILL NEED ADULT ASSISTANCE

Be sure to have help on hand to hang a deer for gutting and **skinning**. A very young hunter will not be able to do this alone. Gutting and skinning can involve a lot of strength to lift a carcass, depending on the size of the deer. Also, don't use sharp knives when alone.

If you decide to take off your jacket for the field dressing process, be sure you are still wearing plenty of the blaze orange color to be safe from other hunters. If possible, you can just push or roll up your sleeves to the elbow. It would be a good idea to wear a blaze orange colored hat. That way, if you need to remove your jacket, you will still be wearing blaze orange on your head.

STARTING THE GUTTING PROCESS

Butchering meat is a delicate and exhausting process.

Begin the field dressing process by making a long slit in the skin or **hide** of the belly. Be careful not to cut too deeply and open up the intestines or the bladder. You don't want feces or urine to contaminate the meat or give it a bad taste. As you slice through the hide, it will contract and draw back from the opening.

Push your fingers under the edges of the split hide and work it away from the muscle and organs. This maneuver will help you work the hide away from the body without puncturing any of the organs such as the intestines.

When you cut far enough up the body to the chest and neck of the animal, you will locate the lungs and windpipe. These can be severed and removed from the body cavity. You will have to slice through various pieces of attaching tissue to loosen the rest of the body parts except the intestines and bladder. Keep working as steadily as you can. Time is not on your side in warmer temperatures over 40 degrees Fahrenheit or 4.4 degrees Celsius.

With a rabbit, bird, or other smaller animal, remove the head first. Taking off the head makes it easier to remove the lungs, heart, and windpipe when f ield dressing.

YOU'RE HALFWAY DONE WITH GUTTING!

After you have removed the windpipe, lungs, heart, liver, and stomach, it's time to remove the intestines and the bladder. You want to be as careful as possible with these organs because of their potentially dangerous contents. When you have removed these parts, the gutting process is finished. If you are field dressing on the ground, prop up the front half of the body to allow the excess blood to drain out of the body cavity. If you want to save the heart and liver for eating, put them into plastic bags and label them with a marker.

Use paper towels to clean up the rest of the blood inside of the body cavity. Don't use old cloth or anything else that may contain bacteria that will contaminate the meat and make it unfit for eating. Be sure to bag the used paper towels for later disposal. Don't leave any litter in the wild.

It's crucial to discard the latex gloves you are wearing. Put the gloves in a plastic bag for disposal and wash your hands carefully. If you have no water in the field, pack some sanitation wipes beforehand to use, and wash your hands well when you get back to camp.

At this point, if you must travel a long way back to camp or home, you can remove the hide, cut up the carcass, and place the different cuts of meat into the plastic bags. Be sure to label them with the marker, so you will remember what part is in each bag when you get back to your camp or home.

If you want to save the head for taxidermy purposes, now is the time to remove it for transportation. Some hunters also keep the hide and have it processed by a taxidermist as well. When removing the head, be careful not to touch the spinal cord because of the threat of chronic wasting disease.

PREPARING THE MEAT

As soon as you arrive at your destination, hang up the carcass. Afterwards, carefully wipe out the inside cavity with a strong saltwater solution to clean away any debris or dirt that may be present. If the animal's feces or urine touched any of the meat, the top layer should be cut away and discarded. It's not sufficient to rinse the area with salt water only. Cut away the meat to avoid any chance of contamination. You don't want to risk getting sick.

Some hunting experts leave the hide on the body until they are ready to remove and divide the meat. If you take the hide off too soon, it will cause the meat to dry out and turn a brown color. After removing the meat from the body, it should be put into a refrigerator or freezer as quickly as possible until you are ready to prepare it for eating.

SKINNING THE CARCASS

Chronic wasting disease affects large numbers of deer and elk.

If you have hung up the carcass by the two hind legs, start the skinning process just below the knees. Cut the hide away from the flesh by separating it from the connective membrane that adheres to the muscle and organs. Scissors can help with this task. In this manner, work your way down the whole body, slicing away the membrane and pulling down the hide until the entire carcass is skinned.

Completely cut the hide from the carcass at the knees and don't go any further down the legs. If you want to mount the head, don't skin the carcass any further than the shoulders, and use a saw to remove the head. If you don't want the head mounted, you can just discard it with the guts and the hide. You will need an adult to help you with this process.

When cutting the carcass into pieces for eating, you need to use a saw for cutting through tough bones. You will need an adult for assistance in this process. Cutting through bone can be difficult for just one person to handle, especially if you are inexperienced.

Venison has been hunted and eaten around the world for centuries.

CHRONIC WASTING DISEASE

Chronic wasting disease, or CWD, has spread through the deer and elk herds of the United States, Canada, and Europe. This illness causes the animal to lose weight, become weak and listless, and eventually die. While hunting deer or elk, it may be difficult to spot if an animal is sick with CWD. However, the hunter can protect themselves from being exposed to the disease by avoiding contact with the animal's brain, spinal cord, or lymph nodes. These are the body parts that CWD affects.

If an animal acts distressed or sick in the wild, or looks too skinny or sick-looking after you have shot it, don't eat the meat. When field dressing a healthy-looking deer, don't touch the parts mentioned above. Study diagrams of a deer or elk's body before you go hunting so you can identify the location of the infected parts. Determining the position of the infected parts will enable you to avoid them when processing the animal for meat.

There is no evidence of chronic wasting disease transferring to a human. However, scientists are still researching the possibility. Be on the safe side, and take the necessary precautions.

DID YOU KNOW?

Deer hunting has been a popular sport since at least the Middle Ages, and remains an important business today.

In Tudor England, venison was so highly prized that the meat was only eaten by kings and high-ranking nobility. Only the very wealthy aristocrats owned forests and hunted deer, so poorer people had no access to venison. Any person of low rank that killed a deer for food was called a "poacher" and either sentenced to having their hands chopped off or put to death.

When English nobility sat down to dinner, they ate deer meat and all sorts of other wild game as well. Their tables overflowed with dishes made from fish, squirrel, bear, blackbirds, turkey, hedgehogs, larks, rabbit, and starlings. Swans were an especially popular delicacy.

Before the Renaissance, European nobility during the Middle Ages enjoyed eating lots of wild game but only very few vegetables. Fruits were not eaten raw but made into pies, sweets, or wine. Poor people only ate meat from domestic animals, such as pigs and cows, which were considered inferior food, as were dairy products such as cheese.

When explorers first landed on the continent of North America, they hunted deer and ate the juicy venison roasted over their campfires. Deer meat formed the basis of their diet just like the Native American and Canadian tribes that lived off the land. The early settlers that later followed the explorers also enjoyed venison because herds of deer were so plentiful. What an odd twist of fate! Back home in England, only nobility could hunt and eat venison, and in America, everyone ate venison every day.

TEXT-DEPENDENT QUESTIONS:

1. Why should a hunter always wear latex or rubber gloves when field dressing a deer?

2. When field dressing an animal, why should you avoid puncturing the intestines and bladder?

3. How can you spot chronic wasting disease or CWD in a deer or elk?

RESEARCH PROJECT:

Interview three hunters to find out their opinion on which is the best way to hang a deer for processing. Do they favor hanging the animal by its feet or by the head? What are the advantages of each method? What are the disadvantages? Compare your findings and write a two-page report on what method you consider to be the best. Also, include research on the pros and cons of having your animal processed commercially. What method do you prefer? What are your reasons for doing so? Read your report to the three hunters. What are their opinions?

 Words to Understand:

brine: A strong salt water solution. Soaking meat in salt water is called brining.

Dutch oven: A cast iron pot with a tight-fitting lid, suitable for cooking over a campfire.

gamey: The name given to wild-harvested meat's unique flavor.

CHAPTER 2
FAMOUS DISHES

THE GAMEY TASTE OF WILD MEAT

Wild animal meat tastes different from domesticated animal meat.

The flavor of wild game is different from that of domesticated animals. Wild animals and birds eat a wide variety of foods in their environment and this gives their meat a unique taste. People describe the taste of wild-harvested meat as "**gamey**." Some love the taste, while others don't like it. However, methods do exist to remove the gamey flavor if you don't like it or you want the cooked food to appeal to more people.

Wild game is always on the move, foraging for food or water, and avoiding predators. This constant exercise makes their flesh very muscular and lean. Livestock raised for food have a much different lifestyle. They are fed regular meals that include hormones and antibiotics and spend their entire lives in pens and other enclosures with no form of exercise. All of these factors make domestic livestock's meat fattier and make it taste different than the flesh of wild game.

PREPARING YOUR WILD GAME FOR THE TABLE

Methods for cooking wild game vary.

There are several ways to process wild-harvested animals and improve the taste of their meat. Two of the most popular methods are using salt water for a **brine** or certain liquids such as vinegar for marinating. When you brine meat, you soak it in a saltwater solution. This process will improve the taste and cause the meat to retain more juiciness during cooking. Marinating the meat uses enzymes to break down the tissues and makes a tough cut of meat more tender and easier to chew. The marinade is made of vinegar and spices and can be used to flavor meat or for older animals with tougher flesh. If the meat contains any fat, cut this off before marinating.

Wild game should be adequately cooked to kill bacteria and parasites, but you must be careful not to overdo it. The overcooked wild game doesn't taste good and becomes tough to chew. That's because wild-harvested meat contains a lot less fat than domestic meat and will dry out quickly when cooked.

Cooking Wild Game: Venison Marsala.

JEAN, VINEGAR, SALT, AND WATER

Sam Carreker hunted every autumn and winter and brought home venison for his wife to prepare for the family. However, his wife, Jean, an adventurous cook that had trained as a chef, never liked the taste of fresh deer meat. She always complained about the "wild, gamey taste," as she described it. However, the rest of the family loved the lean, juicy venison roasts hot out of the oven, surrounded with plenty of potatoes, onions, and carrots.

One day, Jean learned a trick from her uncle, an avid game hunter. He told her to soak the venison in vinegar and salt water overnight before cooking the roast. She tried out his suggestion and loved the result. She said the vinegar and salt water did the trick and the results were amazing! She also occasionally used apple juice which worked well.

PRESERVING MEAT - MAKE JERKY AS THE PIONEERS DID

Making homemade jerky preserves the meat.

Drying and preserving fresh meat makes delicious jerky. You can even make jerky in your camp right after you harvest and field dress the animal by following the instructions below.

For this process, you will need to slice the raw meat very thin. If the sun is out and the day is warm, you can spread the thin strips out in an iron skillet and let it dry out in the sun. Hanging strips of meat on a rack over a low-burning fire will also slowly dry the meat and give it a rich, smoky flavor. You can build a drying rack out of long, green sticks that won't catch fire quickly or buy a rack made for this purpose.

Another way to smoke wild game is to use a tripod to suspend the meat over a low burning fire. You can either make or buy this device. Using a cover over the tripod will contain more smoke to flavor the meat.

Always use hardwoods for smoking meat. Don't use wood from softer trees that contain a lot of sap or resin, such as pine, or this could give an unpleasant flavor to the finished product.

At home, you can make jerky by drying the thin slices of meat in an oven or a dehydrator. If you prefer, you can rub the meat with seasonings or marinade it before the drying process. Freeze the meat beforehand, and it will make slicing the meat into thin slices much easier. Seasonings you can use include any combination of red pepper flakes, soy sauce, garlic, black pepper, paprika, or honey.

PANFRYING MAKES THE QUICKEST MEAL FOR CAMPERS

One of the quickest and tastiest ways of cooking a venison tenderloin steak, a freshly caught fish, or small game bird is to panfry the meat. It's been a classic way to cook in the wild for generations of campers. Many years ago, people in rural areas fried squirrel meat for breakfast after an early morning hunt.

Pan frying outdoors makes a tasty meal.

Clean the meat, fish, or bird very well. Put a small amount of oil in the bottom of a skillet and brown the meat on both sides. When panfrying fish, be careful not to overcook it, or the result will be too dry and tasteless.

An alternative to using oil when panfrying is to fry a couple of pieces of bacon instead and don't drain the grease. Fry the meat in the bacon fat for extra flavor.

RABBIT OR SQUIRREL STEW WITH VEGETABLES - AN OLD FAVORITE

An old-fashioned favorite dish in the eastern United States, rabbit or squirrel stew was a staple for people during the Great Depression when jobs were scarce and food even more so. Squirrels and rabbits were plentiful and easy to hunt.

When cooking a small animal like a rabbit, squirrel, or even an opossum or raccoon, the process is the same. Start out by taking a freshly skinned and dressed animal and washing it well in cold water. After cleaning the carcass, inspect the meat for any remaining fur, dirt, or debris. Cut the carcass into smaller pieces more manageable for eating. Rewash the pieces in cold water. At this point, you may soak the meat in salt water to increase juiciness or a marinade to improve tenderness.

Squirrel pairs well with garlic and butternut squash.

If you will be cooking over a campfire or portable stove, use a cast iron skillet or **Dutch oven** for cooking. Don't use a very high flame for this dish. Remember, you don't want to overcook game, or it ruins the taste.

Mix some flour with herbs or spices (if desired) on a plate and roll the pieces in the mixture until well-coated. Put a small amount of cooking oil in a skillet or Dutch oven and let it heat up for a minute or two. Don't let the oil overheat and start smoking. If the oil begins to smoke, that means the heat is too high.

If you would rather use bacon grease instead of oil, fry three pieces of bacon to flavor your stew. You can discard the fried bacon pieces or just crumble them into the pot after adding the water to the meat.

Lay the meat in the oil and let it cook until light brown. Turn the meat so it browns evenly on all sides. At this point, you don't want to cook the meat all the way, just give it a nicely browned surface. After browning, add enough water to the pan to cover the meat and let it simmer. Add seasonings, such as black pepper, salt, and garlic, but don't do a taste test until the food has cooked for at least 20 minutes. You want to kill any harmful bacteria that may be still lurking on the meat.

Wash and peel as many carrots, potatoes, and onions as needed. Plan on two medium-sized potatoes, two carrots, and half of an onion for each serving. Dice the vegetables up and add to the skillet. Feel free to add other vegetables that you like as well, such as peas or mushrooms. Put a cover on the skillet to keep the water from evaporating too fast as the food cooks.

Keep checking on the food as it cooks. Depending on the temperature of the fire or portable stove flame, it should take about thirty to thirty-five minutes to cook. The meat should be tender and pull away from the bone.

SHEPARD'S PIE - AN ENGLISH FAVORITE WITH A NEW TWIST

Shepard's Pie can be made with a variety of different meats.

If you have any leftover rabbit or squirrel stew, pour it into a baking dish. Use mashed potatoes or a roll-out pastry crust bought at the grocery store to make a top crust. Bake the pie in an oven at 350°F (about 177°C) until the crust is golden brown. You can also make a crust from scratch if you desire.

Frog legs fried in garlic, butter, and lemon creates an excellent dish.

SAM, TURTLE SOUP, AND FROG LEGS

 Sam Carreker hunted all his life since he was seven years old. He had harvested deer, turkey, raccoons, wild boar, doves, squirrels, and rabbits. Growing up near the swamps of the southern United States, two of his favorite dishes were turtle soup and frog legs.

Sam easily caught the turtles in the lake beside his house by baiting a fish hook with chunks of fish. He would clean the turtles, a notoriously hard job, and Jean, his wife, would make them into a creamy soup with butter, garlic, and onions for everyone to enjoy.

Frog legs were hard to acquire. It took a lot of work to catch frogs for dinner. On sultry summer nights, Sam and his daughter would sit out in a small boat on the dark waters of the lake. A small lantern hung from a small pole at the back of the boat. Sam carried a weapon called a frog gig. It looked like a little pitchfork on a very long handle.

Some nights, as Sam and his daughter floated silently along, by the light of the lantern, they saw many frogs leaping along the bank of the lake that rose up like a hill on one side. Sam's hands, a fast blur, speared several frogs and put them in a bucket. His wife Jean would dip the frog legs in a milk and egg mixture, roll them in flour and fry them in butter for dinner. Served with lemon wedges, they tasted delicious.

Sometimes Sam didn't catch any frogs. Sometimes he and his daughter only saw bats flitting overhead, a school of fish, or snakes gliding silently through the water in search of frogs for their dinner. Sometimes they just talked in low voices as they drifted slowly across the moonlit lake and swatted at mosquitoes that whined in their ears. It didn't matter if they caught frogs or not, they enjoyed floating on the lake.

COOKING A LARGE CUT OF VENISON - NORTHERN OR SOUTHWESTERN STYLE

Cooking over an open fire with a Dutch oven adds a unique flavor to any meal.

One of easiest ways to cook a large roast at home is in a slow cooker. Just add the meat and water and cook on low heat for approximately eight hours. The meat will be deliciously tender and juicy. You can add salt and any spice that you like, such as oregano or rosemary, for a distinctive taste. You can also add chili seasoning for a taste of the Southwest. Wash and peel vegetables and add as many as you need per serving to cook with the roast.

If cooking the roast in a Dutch oven, wrapping the meat with slices of uncooked bacon gives the meat a delicious flavor.

MAKE DEER BURGERS!

If you have access to a meat grinder, the kind that's used to make sausage, you can make ground venison for deer burgers. If you don't field dress or butcher your deer, but use a commercial processing plant instead, request some of the meat to be ground like hamburger meat.

Formed into patties and cooked on a grill or outdoor stove, ground deer meat can make some of the most delicious burgers you have tasted. Served on a bun with the usual condiments, such as ketchup, mustard, and a pickle, you will be amazed how good a deer burger tastes.

You don't need beef to make hamburgers. Try it with venison meat.

ROASTING WILD GAME AND VEGETABLES USING ALUMINUM FOIL

Here's another old favorite when it comes to preparing food while camping. The Girl Scouts have used it for many years. It's an easy way to make a satisfying meal while camping. Placed in the coals of the fire, the food will cook inside the foil. All you have to do is slice open the foil, and your food is ready to eat!

Tear off a sheet of foil from the roll and lay it down on your workspace. Don't make the piece of foil too short. It's better to have a piece that is too big than too small for your food. Slice meat and vegetables thinly and layer them on one-half of the piece of foil. An adult will probably need to help with this step. Next, add salt and black pepper, and a small piece of butter. Fold the other half of the foil over your food and fold the edges on all three sides tightly shut. If you have made the piece of foil too short, don't worry. Just unroll another, larger piece and wrap it around your food and the too-short piece as well. Fold the edges tightly together.

Cooking meat in foil tenderizes it.

For cooking meat in foil, you can use any small animal or bird you have cleaned, such as a quail, duck, or goose. If the pieces of meat are small, you won't have to slice it thinly, but if you are using deer or elk meat, slice it thin to speed up the cooking time.

If you would like to use a sauce, such as a barbecue sauce, add as much as you would like. The sauce adds moisture to the foil packets and helps keep the food moist while cooking. Don't add cheese to the food before cooking. The hot temperatures of the coals will cause the cheese to melt and drip out the sides or burn. Remove the packet from the fire after the food has finished cooking. Slit the foil packet open, and add your cheese. The hot temperature of the food will melt the cheese.

Use tongs to handle the foil packets in the fire and be sure never to touch them with your bare hands while hot. Don't place the packets directly on a flaming fire. Use the coals for cooking instead. Let the fire burn down to create a bed of coals. Coals radiate a more even heat, perfect for cooking.

SAFETY WHILE COOKING

Observing safety while cooking is essential because you will be handling sharp knives and working with fire and food at hot temperatures. Don't allow yourself to become distracted and cause an accident. Younger hunters should only cook food over a portable stove or campfire with the supervision of an adult.

Make sure sharp knives are always stored safely and handled with care. If you are unsure how to do something, like slice a venison steak thin for cooking, ask for adult assistance. You should also ask an adult to inspect the wild game meat to make sure it's cooked well enough to kill bacteria and parasites.

Handle knives with care to keep them in good condition and to keep yourself safe from cuts.

DID YOU KNOW?

Ancient Romans had an outrageous taste for wild game. Roman Emperors gave huge feasts with dishes made of camel, parrot heads, dolphin, peacock's tongues, and jellyfish. They also enjoyed seasoning their food with a sauce called garum, made from fermented fish intestines and honey. Garum stank so bad as it fermented that it was unlawful to make it inside of cities!

When exotic animals shipped from foreign lands were killed in the arenas by the gladiators, no meat was wasted. The animal carcasses would be butchered, cooked into a dish, and consumed at big banquets given by the wealthy. Lions, tigers, and even giraffes were all eaten by the rich Romans.

In the American colonies, people had quite a taste for exotic wild game and seafood as well. In the days of George Washington, oyster-flavored ice cream was enjoyed along with other strange desserts such as hot pepper cake. Stewed swan made a favorite dish as well. Pigeons were made into pies and enjoyed by rich and poor alike.

Lobsters, which we consider to be a delicious and expensive treat today, were rejected in the American colonies as being an inferior meat only fed to the lowest citizens, such as prisoners in jails. However, turtle soup was considered a delicacy and favored by the wealthy. American seaport towns, such as Charleston and Savannah, were famous for their turtle soup.

 Words to Understand:

banking: To cover hot coals with ashes to keep them hot.

over the fire grill: A metal grill with legs that will span a fire. It provides a surface to set a pot or cook food directly on the surface.

CHAPTER 3
PAIRING WITH SIDE DISHES

Wild game can be prepared with
a variety of spices and vegetables.

N o meal is complete without side dishes and maybe a sweet dessert. When you are roughing it out in the wild and come back to camp after hunting all day, chances are you will have a ravenous appetite. If you made a kill, you would have fresh meat for your meal, but what goes well with the protein? What is easy and fast to fix?

GIVE A NEW MEANING TO FAST FOOD

You just got back to camp, the sun is setting, and you are starving. How do you feed yourself easily and quickly? What did you pack to bring along on the trip? Do you have any potatoes, carrots, or onions? Did you bring the heavy-duty aluminum foil?

You can use the foil packets described in the last chapter to cook the sides for your meal. You can either cook vegetables with the meat or cook them separately and well seasoned with butter and herbs for a different taste.

Wild Edible Plants in Your Backyard.

BAKED POTATOES IN FOIL

WHAT YOU WILL NEED:

Potatoes (larger ones are best)

Water

Cooking oil or strips of bacon

Heavy duty aluminum foil

Tongs for handling the hot potatoes

Fork to test a potato for doneness

Seasonings such as salt and pepper

Cheese and butter if desired

Potatoes can sometimes take a long time to cook. In a slow-cooker, they can take as long as meat or even longer! Potatoes baked in a bed of coals from a campfire have a great taste, but they may also cook slowly. Start cooking the potatoes before you roast the meat. You can also bake sweet potatoes as well. They don't take as long to cook as a regular potato.

To bake a potato, wrap it in foil and carefully place it directly in the hot coals.

For the first step, wash the potatoes very thoroughly. After washing, let them dry and rub some oil on them. For a more flavorful potato, you can rub the outside with a piece of raw bacon. This keeps the skin of the potato from drying out too much. You can also wrap a piece of bacon around the potato so they will cook together. You can then crumble the bacon onto your sliced open spud for eating.

Wrap the potatoes (with or without the bacon) in foil. Choose a good spot in a bed of coals and bury the potato completely. If the potato is large, it will take an hour or more to cook thoroughly, and a smaller one will take between 30 minutes to 45 minutes. The way to test a baked potato for doneness is to poke it with a fork. If the potato is done, the fork tines will easily pierce the spud. You don't have to unwrap the foil to do this. Push right through the foil with the fork.

Younger hunters should get an adult to help them with burying a potato in a bed of hot coals. It can take some practice to get the potato under the coals and not burn your hand or drop the potato. It can also be difficult to hold the potato with tongs or a long-handled fork.

When the potato is done, push back the coals and pick the potato up with tongs. Be careful that it doesn't drip any hot liquid and cause a painful burn. Let the potato cool for about 15 minutes and then slit open the foil and remove the potato. If you added bacon, pull it away from the potato skin and let it cool for crumbling. At this point, you can cut open the baked potato and add cheese, butter, salt, and pepper.

A campfire is safer when surrounded by rocks.

TIPS FOR USING CAMPFIRE FOR COOKING

When using fire to cook, you should observe a few rules. First, don't build a fire directly on the ground. Dig an appropriately sized hole or pit to contain the blaze. A pit prevents the flames from escaping to the nearby brush and starting a forest fire. Surround the rim of the hole with rock, to further keep the fire from escaping. Having a pit will also contain the coals and ash from the fire which can be useful in maintaining your campfire.

Fires burn out when not attended. When you go to sleep or go out hunting, and no one is around to feed wood to the fire, it will die. The best way to keep a fire alive is to do what is called banking. Covering the fire with ashes to keep it from completely burning out is banking. When a fire is banked, all you have to do is rake back the ash, add more fuel, and the flames will leap up again. To restart a banked fire, don't use large sticks; instead, use small pieces of wood and leaves or pine needles. When the blaze burns high, it's time to add larger pieces of wood.

Banking a fire and restarting it is a lot easier than starting a new blaze from scratch. The coals are already hot and ready to leap back into life when new fuel is added. Banking a fire will save you a lot of time when you are cold and hungry. You can also just cook directly on the coals if you like, instead of using the fire.

Remove the rocks and fill in the fire pit when you are ready to return home. Tamp down the earth to leave the site as you found it. Good hunters are always good caretakers of nature and the earth.

USING AN OVER-THE-FIRE GRILL

Many campgrounds have metal, wood-fed barbecues available.

Steel cooking grills for use over a campfire are very inexpensive. They have folding legs that span the width of the fire, and you can use the top for cooking. These grills can hold skillets and Dutch ovens for cooking almost any kind of food.

COOKING VEGGIES IN A SKILLET

Using a cast-iron skillet adds flavor to a variety of dishes.

Vegetables to use for this dish include squash, zucchini, onions, or mushrooms.

Wash well as many vegetables as needed and pat dry with a paper towel. Chop the veggies into bite-sized pieces. Use a little oil in your skillet, or cook a slice of bacon to produce some grease and flavoring. Put the veggies in the skillet and push around with a fork to keep them from burning as they cook. Add salt, pepper, and other seasonings to taste. When the vegetables soften, they are ready to eat.

CAMPFIRE APPLES IN A SKILLET FOR DESSERT

Try adding apples to your dish for a slightly sweet flavor.

YOU WILL NEED:

Apples

Water

Brown sugar

One tablespoon of butter

Cinnamon, cloves, chopped nuts (optional)

A skillet

Campfire apples are a dessert you can prepare in a skillet over a campfire. Peel as many apples as desired and wash them carefully. Chop the apples into pieces and add to the skillet with approximately a tablespoon of butter. Sprinkle the top of the fruit with enough brown sugar to make the dish as sweet as you wish. Use less sugar if you want the apples to taste more tart. Push the fruit around in the skillet in a continuous motion to coat the apples with butter and prevent the food from burning. When the pieces soften up from the heat, they are ready to eat. Sprinkle the apples with cloves, cinnamon, chopped nuts, or all three ingredients for extra flavor.

WOODEN SKEWERS OR A TOASTING FORK

Steel toasting forks with extendable handles are very useful to have while cooking over a campfire. You can use wooden skewers as well, but keep in mind that wood is flammable.

With a toasting fork, you can make toast for breakfast or hot sandwiches, toast marshmallows for dessert, or roast small bits of meat to add to other dishes, such as baked beans.

BOILED PEANUTS OVER A CAMPFIRE

Boiled peanuts over a campfire make a delicious treat!

It's fun to cook boiled peanuts over a campfire! In the Appalachian Mountains of the United States, it's not an uncommon sight in autumn to see the vendors cooking boiled peanuts in huge metal cauldrons on the side of the road for the tourists. Boiled peanuts make a great appetizer before your main meal.

YOU WILL NEED:

Over-the-fire grill

A big pot with a lid

Water

Dried unroasted peanuts

Salt

A campfire and plenty of firewood

Build a fire in the pit and place the over-the-fire grill across it. Depending on how big of a pot you have, fill it halfway with clean water and the rest of the way with the dried peanuts. Add as much salt as you like, and if you want to make the peanuts Cajun style, add plenty of hot red pepper. Putting a lid on the pot will help conserve the liquid, so you don't have to add water as often.

Depending on the heat of the fire and how many peanuts you are cooking, the peanuts should cook over the fire for anywhere from four to seven hours. This is a wide variance, but each batch is different. When the peanuts no longer float on the water, remove them from the fire.

If you want to try this recipe at home with a slow cooker, let the peanuts cook overnight. The well-done boiled peanut should be soft and mushy inside. Don't drain the water from the peanuts after cooking. The peanuts will continue to soak up the salt and pepper flavoring from the water.

If you have a peanut allergy, please avoid this recipe.

COOK WITH THE SUN

Using the warmth of the sun to help prepare food is a handy technique to learn. It's almost effortless to cook using a solar oven. You can make your own or buy a solar oven from a sporting goods store. The ovens range in price from the small, inexpensive models to the larger and more elaborate. A small model would probably be the best to take on a camping trip.

When cooking with a solar oven, it's best to watch the food for doneness rather than depending on a predetermined cooking time. Conditions can vary from region to region. For instance, cooking with a solar oven in the southern part of Florida would be very different than on the shores of the Great Lakes. The sun's rays are much more intense in Florida, and the food would cook faster.

MAKE SUN TEA

It's easy to make tea on a sunny day. On a hunting trip, you can leave your tea to brew while you are gone.

YOU WILL NEED:

A glass jar with a lid

Water

Teabags

Rinse out the jar and make sure it's clean. Fill the jar with water about three-quarters of the way full. Next, add the tea bags. If you want your tea to be strong, add more tea bags, and if you want it weaker, use less. You will probably need to experiment to get the brew just right for your taste. However, don't worry about making the tea too strong. You can always add more water.

Put the lid on the jar and place in a sunny spot. Between three and five hours are the best to make a full-bodied beverage. However, don't let the tea sit too long in the sun. After too much time, bacteria colonies will start to grow in the tea.

After enough time has passed, remove the jar from the sun and take off the lid. If the tea is too strong for your tastes, now is the time to dilute it with water. Add sugar to the tea, and it's ready to drink. You can add ice if you have it, or just drink the tea warm.

Sun tea makes an excellent addition to any meal.

HOW A SOLAR OVEN WORKS

You can use a solar oven to cook your food if your camp is located in a sunny place. With a solar oven, you won't need to gather any wood and build a fire or use any fuel at all. Solar ovens are very portable, and the simpler versions are inexpensive to buy. They are readily available at sporting goods stores.

If you like to camp and fish in the summer, taking along a solar oven can make cooking the catch of the day quick and easy. Because solar ovens cook with lower temperatures, food doesn't become crispy and brown as it does with conventional cooking methods. However, the lower temperatures help prevent food from burning or drying out too much. This factor makes a solar oven excellent for young hunters just learning how to cook wild game because of its tendency to be overcooked. It's hard to overcook food in a solar oven.

You can use the sun to cook an entire meal!

VENISON ROAST WITH VEGETABLE SIDES IN A SOLAR OVEN

On a sunny day, set up your solar oven and let it preheat in the sunshine.

YOU WILL NEED:

Pot with a lid, such as a Dutch oven

Solar Oven

Venison Roast

Water

Paper towels

Seasoning - salt, pepper, or herbs such as rosemary

Cooking oil or strips of bacon

Onions

Potatoes

Carrots

Wash the roast with water and pat it dry with paper towels. When the venison roast is completely dry, rub the meat with oil and sprinkle with your favorite seasonings. You can also drape several strips of bacon over the roast as well, right over the seasonings.

Place the roast in a pan or dish. Slice onions and pile them around the base of the venison. You can also add other veggies if you would like such as potatoes and carrots. Put the cover on the pot and set it inside the solar oven.

Let the roast cook in the oven for an hour. After that time, check the meat for doneness. If not done, let it cook for another 15 minutes and check again. Keep checking the roast at 15-minute intervals until the roast is finished cooking. When ready, remove the roast from the oven and serve. Be sure to wipe down the inside of the solar oven before you store it.

DID YOU KNOW?

People like to eat strange things. For instance, in Brazil, ants are dipped in chocolate to create a sweet treat.

Several famous people in history enjoyed eating insects. Albert Einstein loved to eat meat throughout his life and did not limit his protein consumption to domestic animals such as beef or chicken. According to varied sources, Einstein would occasionally pick a bug up off the ground and eat it raw.

The French have a long-held tradition of eating a bird called the ortolan, which they eat whole, bones and all. The tiny birds are captured, fattened up and then drowned in a special type of brandy. After being drowned, the birds are plucked and roasted whole. During a meal, the gourmet takes up the bird and eats it whole. Traditionally, the French would eat the ortolan with a napkin draped over the bird's head!

TEXT-DEPENDENT QUESTIONS:

1. What cooks the fastest, potatoes or meat?

2. Why should you dig a pit for a campfire? What are the advantages?

3. What does 'banking a fire' mean?

RESEARCH PROJECT:

Research and build a homemade solar oven. Research several recipes you can cook in your solar oven.

On three sunny days take your oven outside and cook three different dishes. Cook meat on the first day, a vegetable dish the second day, and cook a dish of your choice on the third day. Use a variety of seasonings for each dish.

Did the foods cook in the time expected? Did any factor, such as wind or clouds interfere with the cooking process? How did the food taste after being cooked in the solar oven? Share some of the food with your friends and family. Record their opinions of the food and the solar oven. Write up a report on your findings and present it to your class.

Words to Understand:

algae: A form of plant life without stems and leaves that live in water.

pathogens: Microbes that live in water and make you sick.

CHAPTER 4
LIVING OFF THE LAND

f you learn what plants in your area are edible, you can have a meal anywhere at any time! Many people all over the world eat wild plants, such as stinging nettle, kudzu, pokeweed, and more. Some wild plants are packed with nutrients, vitamins, and minerals even more than domesticated plants.

Wild, edible plants have been used across many
cultures throughout the centuries.

IT'S IMPORTANT TO KNOW YOUR PLANTS

If you learn how to identify local plants that you can eat, it can help you survive in the wild—even if you get lost for an extended period. Learning to identify only a few plants, such as grass, will help you find food to stay alive.

KNOW WHAT YOU CAN EAT

Different people have different physical reactions to plants. It's important for you to determine what plants you can safely eat and which ones may give you a reaction. Do this before going into the wild and eating them when you're perhaps far away from a medical facility. You can test plants, berries, and nuts in the following manner. Wait at least 30 minutes after each step and don't do this alone. Make sure an adult is with you.

Always test for an allergic reaction to a plant before eating it.

Before eating any plant matter, it's important to speak to your parents and a doctor for guidance. Be very careful when trying out plants as food.

To test for a plant, seed, nut, or berry allergy, rub a small piece on your wrist. If there is no adverse reaction after 30 minutes, such as itching or swelling, then rub your lips with the substance. Wait another 30 minutes. Finally, if there is no stinging, itching, or swelling, then take a very tiny taste. If after 30 minutes, there is still no reaction, eat a slightly larger amount and wait an hour. If nothing happens after an hour, you can assume it is safe for you to consume the plant, nuts, seeds, or berries.

If you do have a reaction from plant matter on your wrist or lips, immediately wash the area with warm soap and water and don't eat any of it. Make sure your parents are aware of your reaction.

WILD PLANTS YOU CAN EAT IN THE WILD OR SERVE AS A SALAD

WOOD SORREL AND SHEEP SORREL

There are two types of sorrel good for eating. Wood sorrel is a small plant and looks like clover, with three heart-shaped leaves. Wood sorrel grows in a variety of conditions, anywhere from full sun to shade. A good way of identifying this type of sorrel is from their unique seed pods that look like tiny okra pods. Every part of this plant is edible, and it tastes pleasantly sour.

Wood sorrel is very tasty in a salad or eaten alone. Its slightly lemony taste would go especially well with wild-caught birds or fish.

The second type of sorrel is named sheep sorrel. Sheep sorrel leaves look like elongated arrowheads, and this plant grows close to the ground. It also has a distinctive sour taste like wood sorrel. This plant would also make a delicious salad with a wild, cooked meal.

DANDELION

This so-called weed is highly nutritious and grows almost everywhere. However, don't try to pick dandelion leaves from lawns or near roads or highways sprayed with weed killer.

Spring is probably the best time to gather dandelion leaves for eating when they are very tender. As the leaves age, they can become very bitter-tasting, so always pick the newest leaves for eating.

You can harvest dandelion leaves fresh, wash them in water, and sauté them in butter. They make a great side dish that is highly nutritious as well. Dandelion leaves can be dried and made into a tea, such as sun tea. If you make sun tea from dandelions, you can drink it warm or carry it in your canteen instead of water.

The common dandelion weed is actually edible!

CLOVER

Clover is another plant that's considered a weed and grows almost everywhere. You can add clover to a salad. Clover also has sweet-smelling blooms you can eat.

The white clover flowers in spring make a nice addition to a salad.
Make sure to consult an expert before testing any edible plants.

FINDING WATER IN THE WILD

 The human body needs water more than food to be able to function. Your heart, blood, and lungs depend heavily on having plenty of available water. Running out of water in the wild is dangerous, and finding more should become your top priority if you become lost.

You will need to boil any water before you drink it to kill any harmful pathogens. Boiling is the best and safest way to purify water for drinking. You can also buy commercially produced tablets that will sanitize the water, but you must be careful with the dosage and not use too much.

If you get lost and have no way to purify water, you will need to drink what is on hand regardless of other health issues. The human body can't function longer than a couple of days without water. If you get lost or stranded without any way to purify water, you should drink from flowing water that's clear and clean-looking. Avoid green-looking or stagnant water because it contains algae. Most algae-infested water also contains harmful pathogens.

If it rains, you can trap rainwater to drink or collect the morning dew by soaking up the dew off of plants and wringing out the water into a container.

7 Ways to
Find Water

WILD FOODS YOU CAN EAT IN THE WILD OR SERVE FOR DESSERT

The following are wild fruits and berries that are safe and tasty to eat. You can find these wild foods all over the United States and in Canada.

WILD MUSCADINES

The good thing about the wild muscadine grape, also known as a scuppernong, is they are ripe during deer season in the eastern United States. Walking through the woods in early to late autumn while on a hunt, you can see them hanging from the trees in wooded areas. Wild muscadines may taste a bit sour or tart, or they may taste very sweet depending on the type. They make a tasty meal that you only have to pick and wash.

There is another vine that grows in trees, also in the eastern United States. The vine is called a Virginia Creeper. It also bears dark blue or purplish berries in the autumn, but these are toxic to eat. The Virginia Creeper has five parts to its leaves, and it looks a lot like poison ivy that has three.

Muscadine grapes have a thick skin and a tart flavor.

Sometimes a Virginia Creeper will grow up the same tree as a muscadine grape vine, and the fruit of both vines will mix together. However, a muscadine leaf looks like a traditional grape leaf and nothing like a Virginia Creeper leaf, so be sure to identify what both look like before eating the fruit.

Don't confuse the Virginia Creeper with muscadine grapes.

BLACKBERRIES

Blackberries are another tasty treat that you can eat straight from the vine. Blackberries are also sold in grocery stores so you will be able to identify what the fruit looks like very easily. Blackberries are juicy and sweet and wild varieties usually ripen in June.

Blackberries can be found in the wild.

BLUEBERRIES

Wild blueberries usually ripen in late summer and are very common throughout Maine and Canada where the soil is very acidic. Blueberries are another fruit you can identify by looking at blueberries for sale at your local grocery store. Eat these berries straight from the bush or gather them to serve with your meal.

PASSION FLOWER OR MAYPOP

Maypops are a vine that grows in the eastern part of the United States. Maypops have a beautiful purple and white flower for which it is famous, but the fruit is very delicious too. They grow in dry areas with full sun, such as fields.

Throughout June and July, maypops are ripe. They look like a big green or yellowish colored egg, and if you crack them open, they are filled with seeds much like a pomegranate. Look for maypops that are more yellowish than green. The seeds have a unique taste, sweet and sour at the same time. Served with a meal, they would make a great dessert.

This Maypop is not quite ripe.

WILD PLUMS

Wild plum trees grow all over the United States. They usually grow together in clusters and bear fruit in early summer. The plum is another fruit you can learn to identify by looking at their domestic counterparts in a grocery store. Plums are good eaten raw or sliced open and roasted over a fire. Eating too many wild plums can cause a stomach ache, though.

Wild plums tend to be smaller than those you find in a grocery store.

WILD CRABAPPLE

Here's another fruit that's ripe during deer season in the autumn. Crabapples have leaves that look like a domesticated apple tree, and their fruit is very small and sour. If you're cooking, they are good to chop up and add to pancake or bread batter. Wild crabapples should not be eaten in large quantities or they can cause abdominal distress.

BE SURE BEFORE YOU EAT ANYTHING!

In the beginning, don't just search for edible plants on the Internet and go out and start eating them. You need to be absolutely certain what you are eating. Some poisonous plants look very similar to edible plants. You will need to get confirmation from an expert to make sure a plant is what you think it is before eating it.

Experts in wilderness survival, such as Troop Leaders in the Boy Scouts, may be able to give you reliable advice on what plants can be safely eaten. You can visit state parks and speak with park rangers that may be able to identify edible plants for you. Plant experts at gardening centers may also be able to help.

Park rangers may help you identify edible plants.

LEARNING FROM RELATIVES

 One good thing about having relatives that lived during the Great Depression is how they taught my brothers and me to live off the land. Our relatives said during the Depression hardly anyone where they lived had a job because the companies that employed them had shut down. Americans all over the country were forced to find alternate means of feeding themselves and their families or face the consequence of starving.

During the Great Depression, chicory or even ground acorns were used as a substitute for coffee or to mix with coffee to make it last longer. No clothing was thrown away, just repurposed. Many families, especially in rural areas, depended upon hunting wild game to put meat on the table. Young boys were expected to hunt rabbits or squirrels to help feed the family, or they fished.

Growing up, we learned from our relatives which plants were edible and which ones to avoid. We learned how to walk out in the backyard and find a tasty snack. Some plants taste delicious, while others are an acquired taste.

If you have any relatives that know how to live off the land, pay attention to the lessons they have to teach. You never know when the knowledge will come in handy.

DID YOU KNOW?

Before the rise of modern medicine, healers used many plants as medicine to treat sick people, even if they were known to be toxic. For example, the juice of deadly poppies was traditionally used to deaden pain, and poisonous foxglove helped people with heart problems. Modern pharmacology as we know it today developed from these plants. Many drugs used to treat disease today are still based on plant compounds.

Since ancient times, people depended heavily on different herbs and plants not only to supplement their diet with vitamins and minerals, but to treat disease. In the Medieval times, doctors were extremely few and far between and only worked for the rich and titled. Medical science was also in its infancy, and some of the strange cures the doctors prescribed killed their patients instead of healing them. During the bubonic plague that ravaged the population of Europe and beyond, doctors were virtually helpless.

Everyone else that wasn't wealthy depended upon local wise women to heal the sick. These women diagnosed disease and brewed up concoctions of herbs for medicine. Unfortunately, at various times in history, society turned on these women and accused them of witchcraft. They were prosecuted, driven out of their homes, or put to death. To this day, the image of a witch is associated with a cauldron filled with a bubbling brew, which represents the wise woman of old brewing herbs to cure her patients.

TEXT-DEPENDENT QUESTIONS:

1. What fruits can be found in the wild and safely eaten?

2. How can you positively identify edible plants in the wild?

3. Who treated sick, poor people in Medieval times? What did they use for treatment?

RESEARCH PROJECT:

Research how to make an Underground Still, a survival strategy designed to collect water while you are in the wild. This technique is used by the United States Army and taught to soldiers as part of their survival training. Having knowledge of such a device would help you if you are lost in the wild and need water.

Construct the Underground Still and record how much water you collect in a 24-hour period. Would this be enough water for a human body to survive? Empty the still of water and wait a few days. Collect water from the still again. Did the amount increase or decrease? What factors affect the productivity of the still? Write a report on this project and present it to your class at school.

Briars: A patch of thick underbrush that is full of thorny bushes. Rabbits and other small game love to hide in these.

Burrow: A hole made by a small animal where they live and stay safe from predators. It is also the word for what an animal does when it digs these holes.

Carcass: The dead body of an animal after the innards have been removed and before it has been skinned.

Field dress: To remove the inner organs from an animal after it has been harvested. It's important to field dress an animal as quickly as possible after it has been harvested.

Habitat: The area in which an animal lives. It's important to preserve animal habitats.

Hide: The skin of an animal once it has been removed from the animal. Hides can be made into clothing and other useful gear.

Homestead: A place or plot of land where a family makes their home. This is different from habitat because it is manmade.

Kmph: An abbreviation for kilometers per hour, which is a metric unit of measurement for speed. One kilometer is equal to approximately .62 miles.

Marsh: A wet area of land covered with grasses. The water in a marsh is often hidden by cattail, grasses, and other plants.

Maul: To attack and injure—either an animal or human being can be mauled.

Mph: An abbreviation for miles per hour, which is a unit of measurement for speed. One mile is equal to approximately 1.61 kilometers.

Pepper spray: A chemical used to repel bears and other dangerous creatures. It causes irritation and burning to the skin and eyes.

Poaching: The act of harvesting an animal at a time and place where it is illegal. Always follow the local hunting laws and regulations.

Process a kill: This is when an animal is butchered and cut up into pieces of meat to prepare for cooking. A kill can be processed by yourself or commercially.

Prey: Animals that are hunted for food—either by humans or other animals. It can also mean the act of hunting.

Roosting: What birds do when they rest upon a branch or a tree. Roosting keeps sleeping birds safe from predators.

Scout: To look ahead and observe an area. It is important to scout an area before hunting there. It helps you find evidence of your prey.

Suburbia: The area, people, and culture of a suburban, which is an area outside of a city or town where people live. It is often a small area full of houses.

Swamp: An area of wet land covered in grasses, trees, and other plant life. A swamp is not a good place to build a home, but it can be a good place to hunt.

Thicket: A collection of bushes and branches where small animals, like rabbits and rodents, like to hide.

Timid: A lack of confidence; shy. Rabbits, deer, and birds are often timid, which helps keep them alert and safe from predators.

Vegetation: All of the plant life in an area.

INDEX

FURTHER READING

Fromm, Eric, and Cambronne, Al. *Gut It Cut It Cook It: The Deer Hunters Guide to Processing and Preparing Venison*. Krause Publications. 2009.

Nguyen, Jenny, and Wheatley, Rick. *Hunting for Food: Guide to Harvesting, Field Dressing, and Cooking Wild Game*. F & W Publications. 2015.

Hasheider, Phillip. *The Hunter's Guide to Butchering, Smoking, and Curing*. Voyageur Press, Inc. 2013.

Rinella, Steven. *The Complete Guide to Hunting, Butchering, and Cooking Wild Game, Volume 1: Big Game*. Spiegel & Grau. 2015.

Rinella, Steven. *The Complete Guide to Hunting, Butchering, and Cooking Wild Game, Volume 2: Small Game and Fowl*. Spiegel & Grau. 2015.

INTERNET RESOURCES

www.rabbithuntingonline.com
This is a great site for all kinds of rabbit recipes and info on hunting rabbits.

www.cookwildgame.com
Here you will find lots of recipes for wild game.

www.deeranddeerhunting.com
This site contains plenty of information on deer hunting and venison recipes.

www.pheasantcountry.com
This website has lots of info and interesting recipes for the hunter.

ORGANIZATIONS TO CONTACT

The National Shooting Sports Foundation

Flintlock Ridge Office Center

11 Mile Hill Road

Newton, CT 06470-2359

Phone: (203) 426-1320

Fax: (203) 426-1087

Internet: https://www.nssf.org/

National Firearms Association

P.O. Box 49090

Edmonton, Alberta

Canada T6E 6H4

Phone: 1-877-818-0393

Fax: 780-439-4091

Internet: https://www.nfa.ca

The International Hunter Education Association

800 East 73rd Ave, Unit 2

Denver, Co 80229

Phone: 303-430-7233

Fax: 303-430-7236

Internet: https://www.ihea-usa.org

The National Wildlife Federation

11100 Wildlife Center Drive

Reston, VA 20190

Phone: 1-800-822-9919

Internet: https://www.nwf.org

PHOTO CREDITS

VIDEO CREDITS

Chapter 1
How to Smoke Venison Deer Meat: http://x-qr.net/1G5a

Chapter 2
Cooking Wild Game: Venison Marsala: http://x-qr.net/1DQK

Chapter 3
Wild Edible Plants in Your Backyard: http://x-qr.net/1H4D

Chapter 4
7 Ways to Find Water: http://x-qr.net/1Dmr

AUTHOR'S BIOGRAPHY

Elizabeth Dee has hunted extensively in the southeast part of the United States for small and large game. She has also cleaned and cooked game for family meals. Elizabeth has been writing for over 25 years for magazines and web articles.